WHAT THE BIBLE SAYS ABOUT

Prayer

ROSE
PUBLISHING

Torrance, California

What the Bible Says about Prayer
© 2015 Bristol Works, Inc.

Rose Publishing, Inc.
4733 Torrance Blvd., #259
Torrance, California 90503 USA
www.rose-publishing.com

Contributors: Jessica Curiel, MA; William Brent Ashby, BT

Special thanks to: Laura Grove

Printed in the United States of America
010915RRD

Contents

Before You Pray

At its base, prayer is talking with God. We can pray alone or in a group; silently or aloud; using a written prayer or a spontaneous one. But to be in prayer is more than just speaking words. Scripture portrays a life of continual prayer, meaning a kind of openness toward God in all we do (1 Thessalonians 5:17). Our entire lives should be prayers to God, exhibiting the praise and love of our Creator and Savior.

Here are three things you need to know before you pray.

1. **GOD CARES FOR YOU.**

Because of God's unfailing love for us, we can bring anything and everything in our hearts to God in prayer. Prayer is a safe place of trust.

> *Cast all your anxiety on him because he cares for you.*
> —1 Peter 5:7

> *I trust in God's unfailing love for ever and ever.* —Psalm 52:8

2 GOD HEARS YOUR PRAYERS.

God Almighty is listening. Because we are his beloved children, no prayer is too small for him to hear.

> *He will listen to the prayers of the destitute. He will not reject their pleas.* —Psalm 102:17 NLT

> *How gracious he will be when you cry for help! As soon as he hears, he will answer you.*
> —Isaiah 30:19

> *For the eyes of the Lord are on the righteous and his ears are attentive to their prayer.*
> —1 Peter 3:12a

3. YOU CAN PRAY WITH CONFIDENCE.

You don't have to be a prayer giant to come confidently to God in prayer. As believers, we can all equally approach God because of our unique standing in Jesus.

> *In him [Jesus] and through faith in him we may approach God with freedom and confidence.*
> —Ephesians 3:12

Let us then approach God's throne of grace with confidence, so that we may receive mercy and find grace to help us in our time of need.

—Hebrews 4:16

Prayer should not be regarded "as a duty which must be performed, but rather as a privilege to be enjoyed, a rare delight that is always revealing some new beauty."

—E. M. Bounds

Why Pray

PRAYER IS IMPORTANT.

God's Word instructs believers to make prayer a high priority. God wants to hear from his children.

> *Devote yourselves to prayer.*
> —Colossians 4:2

> *I urge, then, first of all, that petitions, prayers, intercession and thanksgiving be made for all people. ... Therefore I want the men everywhere to pray, lifting up holy hands without anger or disputing.* —1 Timothy 2:1, 8

PRAYER DRAWS US CLOSE TO GOD.

In prayer, we worship, confess our sins, bring our requests to God, and wait and listen for him to speak. In short, we enter deeply and directly into relationship with God. Through communion with God, our hearts and minds will be changed to be more like our Lord, and we will grow to know his perfect will for our lives.

> *Do not conform to the pattern of this world, but be transformed by the renewing of your mind. Then you will be able to test and approve what God's will is—his good, pleasing and perfect will.*
> —Romans 12:2

> *So all of us who have had that veil removed can see and reflect the glory of the Lord. And the Lord—who is the Spirit—makes*

us more and more like him as we are changed into his glorious image. —2 Corinthians 3:18 NLT

PRAYER IS POWERFUL.

God not only hears our prayers, but he is acting on them. Our prayer requests bring about real change in the world and in the lives of the people we pray for.

"Ask and it will be given to you; seek and you will find; knock and the door will be opened to you. For everyone who asks receives; the one who seeks finds; and to the one who knocks, the door will be opened." —Matthew 7:7–8

"If you believe, you will receive whatever you ask for in prayer." —Matthew 21:22 (Mark 11:24; John 15:7, 16)

And the prayer offered in faith will make the sick person well. ... The prayer of a righteous person is powerful and effective.
—James 5:15–16

Dear friends, if our hearts do not condemn us, we have confidence before God and receive from him anything we ask, because we keep his commands and do what pleases him. —1 John 3:21–22

"Prayer is a strong wall and fortress of the church; it is a goodly Christian weapon."

—Martin Luther

PRAYER BRINGS PEACE.

When we are at our wit's end, Scripture tells us to turn all those anxieties over to God who will give us peace of mind.

> *Do not be anxious about anything, but in every situation, by prayer and petition, with thanksgiving, present your requests to God. And the peace of God, which transcends all understanding, will guard your hearts and your minds in Christ Jesus.* —Philippians 4:6–7

PRAYER PROTECTS US.

We have Almighty God on our side! Jesus showed believers the importance of praying for protection and deliverance. (Also see 2 Corinthians 10:4; Ephesians 6:10–18.)

Jesus' prayer for his disciples:

> *"My prayer is not that you take them out of the world but that you protect them from the evil one."* —John 17:15

The Lord's Prayer:

> *"And lead us not into temptation, but deliver us from the evil one."*
> —Matthew 6:13

Jesus warns his disciples:

> *"Keep alert at all times. And pray that you might be strong enough to escape these coming horrors and stand before the Son of Man."* —Luke 21:36 NLT

"Prayer as a relationship is probably your best indication about the health of your love relationship with God. If your prayer life has been slack, your love relationship has grown cold."

—John Piper

How to Pray

Sometimes, learning about the heroes of the faith is intimidating. Instead of being motivated to pray and have a faith like theirs, we feel discouraged with the enormous challenge of their example. But who could fly a jet or run a marathon without much previous and rigorous training? It's the same with prayer. No one is born knowing how to pray and being great at it. Learning to pray is a bit like learning to swim. It can only happen in the water, despite fears, insecurities, and doubts.

Here are some helpful things to keep in mind as you learn to pray:

1. Prayer requires concentration and focus. Teaching ourselves to concentrate is one of the reasons we close our eyes. But we need to close our ears and minds as well to the many distractions around us. Spending a few minutes just to quiet mind and heart will help us achieve better concentration and focus.

2. Prayer builds up our humility, dependence on God, and compassion for others. If praying on your own is difficult, make a "prayer date" with a friend you are comfortable with.

3. Start by praying simple, short prayers—pray one minute, take a break and read or sing, then pray again. When you feel stuck,

unmotivated, or without words—all very normal occurrences—pray a prayer from the Bible:

- A psalm (For example, Psalm 6, 23, or 86)

- Nehemiah's prayer (Nehemiah 1:5–11)

- The Lord's Prayer (Matthew 6:9–13)

- Solomon's prayer (1 Kings 8:22–61)

4. Your prayers do not have to be pretty. The Holy Spirit takes all of our prayers, pretty or not, and brings them before God the Father (Romans 8:26–27).

5. Make sure your prayers include, among other things, praise for God's greatness, gratitude for God's gifts, petitions for you and others, confession of your struggles and

sins, and whatever the Spirit brings to your mind.

6. Sometimes prayer is a battleground. Prayer can be difficult and produce anxiety. Sometimes it is while praying that God reveals to us what needs changing and what needs to be done. Prayer can be a painful mirror.

7. Finally, our prayers are not primarily for changing God's mind about something. Prayer changes our mind about who we are, what we need, and how we please God. Prayer is transformational.

"The battle of prayer is against two things in the earthlies: wandering thoughts, and lack of intimacy with God's character as revealed in His word. Neither can be cured at once, but they can be cured by discipline."

—Oswald Chambers

PRAY ALWAYS.

We should live in a constant attitude of prayer. John MacArthur, a Christian author and pastor, explains that praying continually means "you live your life and your experiences of life with a constant, close connection to the Lord and are drawn into his presence through everything." (Also see Psalm 1; Joshua 1:8.)

Rejoice always, pray continually [or "pray without ceasing"], give thanks in all circumstances; for this is God's will for you in Christ Jesus. —1 Thessalonians 5:16–18

"No learning can make up for the failure to pray. No earnestness, no diligence, no study, no gifts will supply its lack."

—E. M. Bounds

In all requests, we should keep the perspective that it is always if the Lord wills. He is still in charge and knows best.

> Now listen, you who say, "Today or tomorrow we will go to this or that city, spend a year there, carry on business and make money." Why, you do not even know what will happen tomorrow. ... Instead, you ought to say, "If it is the Lord's will, we will live and do this or that." —James 4:13–15

> This is the confidence we have in approaching God: that if we ask anything according to his will, he hears us. And if we know that he hears us—whatever we ask— we know that we have what we asked of him. —1 John 5:14–15

PRAY IN THE HOLY SPIRIT.

Every time you pray, come with an open heart allowing God's Spirit in you to guide your prayers. Where we are inadequate, the Spirit knows exactly the right thing to say. (Also see Romans 8:15–16; Ephesians 5:18.)

> *Pray in the Spirit at all times and on every occasion. Stay alert and be persistent in your prayers for all believers everywhere.*
> —Ephesians 6:18 NLT

> *But you, dear friends, must build each other up in your most holy faith, pray in the power of the Holy Spirit, and await the mercy of our Lord Jesus Christ, who will bring you eternal life. In this way, you will keep yourselves safe in God's love.* —Jude 20–21 NLT

We do not know what we ought to pray for, but the Spirit himself intercedes for us through wordless groans. And he who searches our hearts knows the mind of the Spirit, because the Spirit intercedes for God's people in accordance with the will of God. —Romans 8:26–27

ASK IN FAITH—AND ALSO FOR FAITH.

Faith may move mountains, but having that faith is often easier said than done. The Gospel of Mark tells a story of a father who wanted to fully believe that Jesus would answer his request to heal his son. The father cried out to Jesus, "I do believe; help me overcome my unbelief!" Even though this man had difficulty with faith, Jesus healed his son (Mark 9:14–29). Like this father, we too can pray for stronger faith.

Jesus replied, "Truly I tell you, if you have faith and do not doubt, not only can you do what was done to the fig tree, but also you can say to this mountain, 'Go, throw yourself into the sea,' and it will be done. If you believe, you will receive whatever you ask for in prayer." —Matthew 21:21–22

If any of you lacks wisdom, you should ask God, who gives generously to all without finding fault, and it will be given to you. But when you ask, you must believe and not doubt, because the one who doubts is like a wave of the sea, blown and tossed by the wind. That person should not expect to receive anything from the Lord. —James 1:5–7

PRAY IN JESUS' NAME.

Jesus' death on the cross removed the "sin block" for all who believe. The lines of communication are now open for those who trust in Christ. This is what it means to pray in Jesus' name, for only through Jesus will any prayer be heard by God.

To pray in Jesus' name is to pray in the authority of that name, much as we might use the phrase "in the name of the law" to assert the authority of the law. But the use of Jesus' name should be more than a mere postscript on our prayers, more even than an authoritative letterhead. To pray effectively in Christ's name, we must be "in him"—in union with his life and death.

Praying in Jesus' name does not give our prayers extra power. The truth is, prayers are completely powerless in the first place unless they are "in Jesus."

Without Christ's intercession, no prayers would make it to the ears of God. The reason we are told to pray in and by his authority is not as some magic formula, but to put our own spirits and our own thinking in the right place—under and in him.

> *"I am the vine; you are the branches. If you remain in me and I in you, you will bear much fruit; apart from me you can do nothing. … You did not choose me, but I chose you and appointed you so that you might go and bear fruit—fruit that will last—and so that whatever you ask in my name the Father will give you." —John 15:5, 16*

> *"Until now you have not asked for anything in my name. Ask and you will receive, and your joy will be complete." —John 16:24*

PRAY WITH A CLEAR MIND AND SELF-CONTROL.

The end of all things is near. Therefore be alert and of sober mind so that you may pray.
—1 Peter 4:7

PRAY IN AGREEMENT WITH OTHER BELIEVERS.

"Again, truly I tell you that if two of you on earth agree about anything they ask for, it will be done for them by my Father in heaven. For where two or three gather in my name, there am I with them." —Matthew 18:19–20

KEEP ON PRAYING.

Persevere as you wait for the Lord to answer. Pray and don't give up.

Be joyful in hope, patient in affliction, faithful in prayer.
—Romans 12:12

FOUR KINDS OF PRAYER

There are many types of prayer. Here are several main categories of prayer. A person may pray one or all of these in a single prayer time, and in any order. You can remember these categories with the acronym ACTS.

Adoration

Confession

Thanksgiving

Supplication

Adoration

Prayer, first and foremost, ought to be about worship. God alone is worthy of undiluted praise. That would be true even if God never gave us a thing, and that is why adoration is distinct from thanksgiving.

Notice that the Lord's Prayer begins with "Our Father in heaven, hallowed be your name" (Matthew 6:9). Holding up God's name for praise is our prime duty in prayer.

Examples: 1 Chronicles 29:10; 2 Chronicles 6:26–27; Luke 2:37.

Confession

"Forgive us our sins, for we also forgive everyone who sins against us" (Luke 11:4). Knowing that human sin blocks communication with God, Jesus taught his disciples to pray this way to make sure that there were no stumbling blocks between God and them.

Examples: 2 Chronicles 7:14; Daniel 9:4–19; 1 John 1:8–9.

Thanksgiving

Thanksgiving is praise for something God has done for us or given to us—or for what we trust him to do.

The apostle Paul thanked God for the believers in Philippi:

> *I thank my God every time I remember you. In all my prayers for all of you, I always pray with joy because of your partnership in the gospel from the first day until now.* —Philippians 1:3–5

Examples: Psalm 100:4; 107:1; 118:21; Matthew 14:19; Ephesians 1:15–16; 1 Thessalonians 1:2; 5:16–18; 1 Timothy 4:4.

Supplication
(Also called Petition)

Our heavenly Father wants his children to bring their requests to him (Philippians 4:6).

Jesus taught:

> *"If you, then, though you are evil, know how to give good gifts to your children, how much more will your Father in heaven give good gifts to those who ask him!"*
> —Matthew 7:11

Intercession is a type of supplication where we pray for the needs and concerns of others. And we should not just pray for our friends, but also "pray for those who persecute you" (Matthew 5:44).

Examples: Genesis 24:12–15; 1 Samuel 7:8.

"Don't pray when you feel like it. Have an appointment with the Lord and keep it. A man is powerful on his knees."

—Corrie Ten Boom

How Not to Pray

God does not expect us to be perfect to come to him in prayer, but he does expect us to be honest. Prayer should be the place where we meet God honestly and openly. The Bible tells us that the prayers that God does not accept are the prayers of hypocrisy.

PRAYERS THAT ARE SPOKEN TO PAT OURSELVES ON THE BACK.

Jesus' parable of the Pharisee and the tax collector shows the difference between a prayer that comes from a heart of arrogance and one that comes from humility.

> *"Two men went up to the temple to pray, one a Pharisee and the other a tax collector. The Pharisee stood by himself and prayed: 'God, I thank you that I am not like other people—robbers, evildoers, adulterers—or even like this tax collector. I fast twice a week and give a tenth of all I get.' But the tax collector stood at a distance. He would not even look up to heaven, but beat his breast and said, 'God, have mercy on me, a sinner.' I tell you that this man, rather than the other, went*

home justified before God. For all those who exalt themselves will be humbled, and those who humble themselves will be exalted." —Luke 18:9–14

PRAYERS THAT ARE PRAYED ALL THE WHILE IGNORING GOD'S INSTRUCTIONS.

God cares about whether we are following him and how we are treating others, rather than if we are simply going through the motions of prayer. Those prayers end up being empty and hindered.

> *If anyone turns a deaf ear to my instruction, even their prayers are detestable.* —Proverbs 28:9

> *For I desire mercy, not sacrifice, and acknowledgment of God rather than burnt offerings.*
> —Hosea 6:6

Husbands, in the same way be considerate as you live with your wives, and treat them with respect as the weaker partner and as heirs with you of the gracious gift of life, so that nothing will hinder your prayers. —1 Peter 3:7

See also Psalm 66:18–20.

"We may pray most when we say least, and we may pray least when we say most."

—Augustine of Hippo

PRAYERS THAT ARE FOR SELFISH REASONS.

God knows all desires and no secret is hidden from him. Real prayer is an attitude of the heart.

> *You desire but do not have, so you kill. You covet but you cannot get what you want, so you quarrel and fight. You do not have because you do not ask God. When you ask, you do not receive, because you ask with wrong motives, that you may spend what you get on your pleasures.* —James 4:2–3

See also 1 Thessalonians 5:16–18.

PRAYERS THAT ARE LONG AND LOUD TO GET ATTENTION AND ADMIRATION FROM OTHER PEOPLE.

"When you pray, don't be like the hypocrites who love to pray publicly on street corners and in the synagogues where everyone can see them. I tell you the truth, that is all the reward they will ever get. But when you pray, go away by yourself, shut the door behind you, and pray to your Father in private. Then your Father, who sees everything, will reward you. When you pray, don't babble on and on as people of other religions do. They think their prayers are answered merely by repeating their words again and again. Don't be like them, for your Father knows exactly what

you need even before you ask him!" —Matthew 6:5–8 NLT

See also Mark 12:40 and Luke 20:47.

Unanswered Prayers

WHEN GOD SAYS NO

Anyone who has made prayer a part of his or her life knows that not everything asked for in prayer is granted. Prayer requests are just that—requests; not demands or magic words that will make something happen. God hears our prayers and makes them effective, but he ultimately decides how to answer them—and sometimes that answer is no.

"No" is one of the shortest yet hardest words to hear. But what does God's "no" mean? Often his "no" is not a "No way!" or "Forget about it," but rather it is, "No, I have something better in mind."

Moses

Moses asked to cross over the Jordan River to see the Promised Land. God said "No," but he let Moses view the land from the top of a mountain.

> At that time I pleaded with the Lord: "Sovereign Lord ... Let me go over and see the good land beyond the Jordan — that fine hill country and Lebanon." But because of you the Lord was angry with me and would not listen to me. "That is enough," the Lord said. "Do not speak to me anymore about this matter. Go up to the top of Pisgah and look west

*and north and south and east.
Look at the land with your own
eyes, since you are not going to
cross this Jordan. But commission
Joshua, and encourage and
strengthen him, for he will lead
this people across and will cause
them to inherit the land that you
will see."* —Deuteronomy 3:23–28

David

King David asked to set up God's
temple. God said "No," but promised
to set up David's kingdom forever, and
later allowed David's son, Solomon, to
build God's temple.

*David rose to his feet and said:
"My brothers and my people!
It was my desire to build a
Temple where the Ark of the
Lord's Covenant, God's footstool,
could rest permanently. I made*

the necessary preparations for building it, but God said to me, 'You must not build a Temple to honor my name, for you are a warrior and have shed much blood. ... Your son Solomon will build my Temple and its courtyards, for I have chosen him as my son, and I will be his father.'"

—1 Chronicles 28:2–3, 6 NLT

Mary and Martha

Mary and Martha asked Jesus to come quickly and heal their dying brother, but instead Jesus waited until their brother died. Then Jesus did something beyond their wildest expectations: he raised their brother from the dead! He answered their hearts' longing in a different way than what they had asked for.

> Then Jesus said, "Did I not tell you that if you believe, you will see the glory of God?"
> —John 11:40

Paul

Paul pleaded three times for God to free him from a problem (the "thorn in his flesh"), but God did not remove it. However, through accepting the problem, Paul found that God's grace was sufficient for him and that power is made perfect in weakness. Paul found a greater meaning in his unanswered prayer.

> *Three times I pleaded with the Lord to take it away from me. But he said to me, "My grace is sufficient for you, for my power is made perfect in weakness." Therefore I will boast all the more gladly about my weaknesses, so that Christ's power may rest on me.* —2 Corinthians 12:8–9

Jesus

Jesus' prayer in the Garden of Gethsemane is the only prayer Jesus made that was denied. He prayed that, if it were possible, the suffering he was about to experience would be avoided. Yet he also prayed, "not my will, but yours be done." This example should teach us that there are some things we ask for—good as they may seem—that are not God's will for us. Jesus accepted the Father's will that he should suffer on our behalf. And just look at the powerful results: the forgiveness of sins and Jesus' resurrection from the dead! In Jesus' case, as in ours, the ultimate outcome from God will be life out of death.

> *Going a little farther, [Jesus] fell with his face to the ground and prayed, "My Father, if it is possible, may this cup be taken from me. Yet not as I will, but as you will."* —Matthew 26:39

See also Matthew 26:36–42; Mark 14:32–36; Luke 22:39–44; John 18:11

"*God's answers are wiser than our prayers.*"

—Anonymous

WHEN GOD SEEMS SILENT

Sometimes we pray for change in our lives or the lives of our loved ones, and yet nothing happens. We do what we can, but God seems silent. From our perspective, our prayers may look like they are falling on deaf ears. Should we keep praying? Jesus addresses this important concern through two parables.

The Parable of the Friend in Need

Luke 11:5–13

After Jesus teaches his disciples how to pray in the Lord's Prayer, he continues to instruct them through a story about a man who needs to borrow some food from a friend late at night for a visitor who is coming. Jesus says that the man will receive what he needs from his friend, not because his friend is so generous, but simply because of the man's persistence and boldness.

The Lesson: God, who is far more generous than the friend, will surely supply our needs if we consistently ask him.

The Parable of the Persistent Widow

Luke 18:1–8

"Jesus told his disciples a parable to show them that they should always pray and not give up" (v. 1). In this parable, a widow keeps coming back day after day to seek justice from a corrupt judge. Though the judge does not care about the woman's concern, he gets tired of her bothering him, so he grants her justice.

The Lesson: If even a corrupt judge grants persistent requests, how much more will God who is just and cares for us bring about justice in our lives when we continue to call on him.

"Prayer does not mean simply to pour out one's heart. It means rather to find the way to God and to speak with him, whether the heart is full or empty."

—Dietrich Bonhoeffer

WAITING FOR GOD TO ANSWER

As we pray for all the things we want and need and hope for, we must remember that prayer involves learning what God wants for our lives. When we make God our top priority in prayer, our will begins to align with his will. As we stay connected to God, he will transform our hearts to his will. (See John 15.)

> *"But seek first his kingdom and his righteousness, and all these things will be given to you as well."* —Matthew 6:33 (Luke 12:31)

> *Take delight in the LORD, and he will give you the desires of your heart. ... Be still before the LORD and wait patiently for him.*
> —Psalm 37:4, 7a

One thing I ask from the Lord, this only do I seek: that I may dwell in the house of the Lord all the days of my life, to gaze on the beauty of the Lord and to seek him in his temple. —Psalm 27:4

The Lord's Prayer

When Jesus' disciples wanted to know how to pray, he taught them a prayer that is known today as "The Lord's Prayer." But this prayer is not so much Jesus' prayer as it is our prayer—it is how Jesus wants all his followers to pray.

Jesus said:

This, then, is how you should pray:

Our Father in heaven,
hallowed be your name,
your kingdom come,
your will be done,
on earth as it is in heaven.

Give us today our daily bread.

*And forgive us our debts,
as we also have forgiven our
debtors.*

*And lead us not into temptation,
but deliver us from the evil one.*

—Matthew 6:9–13 (See also
Luke 11:2–4)

Jesus provided his followers with guidelines for prayer based on the attributes or characteristics of God. The two main sections of the prayer divide with the words "your" and "us."

1. The first part centers on God, putting God in his rightful place in our priorities. Only by focusing on the patient and loving Father can we find the attitude that puts our own needs in perspective.

2. The second part focuses on our needs—body, soul, and spirit—and the needs of others. In just three brief requests, Jesus targets all of human behavior and character and reminds us that we always need him. Only in moment-by-moment dependence on God will we experience the good things God wants to provide.

THE SEVEN PETITIONS OF THE LORD'S PRAYER

"Your"

PETITION #1: Our Father in heaven, hallowed be your name.

God's holiness comes first. To hallow means to make holy. To hallow God's name means to honor it as holy and sacred. When we pray, we enter the presence of God with reverence, worship, and thanksgiving. We thank God not only for what he has done, but also for who he is. God's greatness and glory alone are worthy of praise and thankfulness. Thanksgiving recognizes that everything we have belongs to God, whether it's our talents, possessions, jobs, or children.

God is a loving and compassionate Father who gives life, provides for, and protects those who trust him. Like a caring human father, God wants a close relationship with his children. Addressing God as "Our Father" plunges the person praying into a relationship. A child approaching a loving father knows that his or her father will give careful attention to the child's requests and will be lovingly inclined towards the child's best interests. The child knows that the father will answer. This is how Jesus tells us to approach God—as trusting children of a patient, tender father.

PETITION #2: *Your kingdom come.*

God's sovereignty is a fact affirmed by believers. We pray for the day when the world will see God's rule. God has supreme power and authority over everything in heaven and earth. When we acknowledge God's sovereignty, we affirm and welcome his reign in our lives. We promise to live in ways that honor him.

God's kingdom is both here and now—and yet to come. During Jesus' life on earth, his ministry was "to proclaim good news to the poor. He has sent me to proclaim freedom for the prisoners and recovery of sight for the blind, to set the oppressed free, to proclaim the year of the Lord's favor" (Luke 4:18–19). When Jesus was around, people were freed from sickness, suffering, and pain. When Jesus returns to reign supreme, there will be no pain, suffering, or evil ever again. God will make everything right in the end.

PETITION #3: *Your will be done, on earth as it is in heaven.*

God's authority extends over all his creation. We pray for his authority to be known and obeyed in all the earth.

God's perfect will is always being done in heaven. But on earth, human free will results in selfishness, greed, and evil. In this part of the Lord's Prayer, we ask that God's will would take place on earth. More specifically, we pray for God's will to become our will. God calls each one of his children to live rightly and do good to others, caring for those around us as much as for ourselves. We pray that all people submit to the will of God over their own desires and faithfully love God and neighbors as themselves. Relationship with God depends on obedience to his will. God's will should be the context for everything we ask for, say, and do.

"Us"

Petition #4: Give us today our daily bread.

God's providence for our daily needs means that we may pray in faith that God will provide what we need or a way to obtain what we need.

God is able to provide for all our needs. The Greek word for "bread" represents not just food, but every physical thing we need. When we pray for our daily bread, we ask God to provide for our material, physical, emotional, relational, and spiritual needs for that day. Daily bread can include the daily needs of ministries, people, communities, leaders, family, friends, as well as personal needs. God commits himself to provide for his children, yet God knows more about what we need than we ourselves know. By praying for daily bread, we are not taking it for granted, but acknowledging that all our life depends on his mercy.

PETITION #5: *And forgive us our debts, as we also have forgiven our debtors.*

God's forgiveness of our sins (debts) is possible because of Jesus' sacrifice on the cross. We ask God to forgive the wrong we have done as well as our neglect of the good things we should have done. But there is a catch: God will forgive us only as much as we forgive those who have injured us. God is merciful and he expects us to be also. If we refuse to forgive others, how can we expect God's forgiveness? We can expect to see God's mercy in our lives according to how merciful we are to others (Mark 11:25).

Petition #6: And lead us not into temptation.

God's protection from the things that will trip us up and undo us is something we need to ask for. Whether in trial or out of trial, we should seek God's protection.

Petition #7: But deliver us from the evil one.

God's deliverance from enemies and especially from death and the Devil are legitimate concerns. We are taught to pray that we won't be tempted to do wrong. In a practical way, this is like praying that God will keep our minds off of tempting situations.

People used to excuse bad behavior by saying, "The Devil made me do it." But in reality, the devil cannot make us do wrong. We do it ourselves. God won't make us obey him, but he does give us the power to walk away from wrong choices. The Holy Spirit gives us strength to withstand temptation, avoid sin, and strive for holiness. Satan is constantly seeking to attack the hearts and minds of those who love God. God provides us with the defenses we need to protect ourselves against the weapons of Satan. By praying for protection, we prepare each day for battle against evil. We can be confident in our prayers for deliverance because we are more than conquerors through Christ (Romans 8:37).

"We pray for the big things and forget to give thanks for the ordinary, small (and yet really not small) gifts."

—Dietrich Bonhoeffer

Prayers in the Bible

The Bible provides us with many examples of all kinds of people praying for all sorts of things—in all imaginable situations! These examples show us that we can pray anytime and anywhere. Here's the *who, what, where, when, why,* and *how* of prayers in the Bible.

WHO PRAYED?

A national leader (Moses)
Exodus 32:11–13, 31–32;
Numbers 14:13–19

A child (Samuel)
1 Samuel 3:10

A military commander (Joshua)
Joshua 7:6–9

A weak man, once strong (Samson)
Judges 16:28

A childless wife (Hannah)
1 Samuel 1:10–11

Priests
2 Chronicles 30:27

Foreigners from distant lands
2 Chronicles 6:32–33

An elderly widow (Anna)
Luke 2:36–38

A man on his deathbed (Hezekiah)
Isaiah 38:2–3

A prophet (Isaiah)
Isaiah 6:8

A king and musician (David)
Psalm 139

A grieving man (Jeremiah)
Lamentations 3

A rebellious man (Jonah)
Jonah 2:2–9

Frightened sailors
Jonah 1:14

An elderly priest (Zechariah)
Luke 1:13

A blind beggar (Bartimaeus)
Mark 10:47

Jesus' family (his brothers and mother)
Acts 1:14

The Son of God
John 17

A seeking Gentile (Cornelius)
Acts 10:31

Widows
1 Timothy 5:5

Worshipers in heaven
Revelation 11:15–18

WHY DID THEY PRAY?

Were afraid for their life (Moses)
Exodus 17:4–5

Felt betrayed by God (Moses)
Numbers 11:10–15

A sister was ill (Moses for Miriam)
Numbers 12:13

Feared enemy nations (Joshua)
Joshua 6–8

Wanted revenge (Samson)
Judges 16:28

Experienced life-changing disasters
(Job)
Job 1:20–21

Were thankful to God for a child
(Hannah)
1 Samuel 2:1–10

Saw God fulfill his promise (Solomon)
1 Kings 8:23–53

Didn't know what to do (Jehoshaphat)
2 Chronicles 20:1–12

Couldn't go on anymore (Elijah)
1 Kings 19:4

Had a big decision and move to make (Nehemiah)
Nehemiah 2:4

Were very depressed
Psalm 116:3–4

A boy was demon possessed (Jesus' teaching about the need for prayer)
Mark 9:29

Had new church leaders appointed
Acts 6:6; 14:23

Were thankful for other believers (Paul)
Ephesians 1:16; 1 Thessalonians 1:2

A woman had died (Peter for Tabitha)
Acts 9:40–42

A father was ill (Paul for Publius's father)
Acts 28:8

Were awaiting the Lord's return (John)
Revelation 22:20

He who testifies to these things says, "Yes, I am coming soon." Amen. Come, Lord Jesus.

—Revelation 22:20

WHAT DID THEY PRAY FOR?

To spare a wicked city (Abraham for Sodom)
Genesis 18:23–25

A bride (Abraham's servant)
Genesis 24:12–14

Protection from a brother (Jacob)
Genesis 32:9–12

Their grandsons (Jacob)
Genesis 48:15–16

Someone else to do the work (Moses)
Exodus 4:13

To see God (Moses)
Exodus 33:18

To see the Promised Land (Moses)
Deuteronomy 3:23–25

A child to be raised from the dead (Elijah for a widow's son)
1 Kings 17:21

Parenting instructions (Samson's father)
Judges 13:8

A sign from God (Gideon)
Judges 6:17–18

More sunlight (Joshua)
Joshua 10:12

A son (Hannah)
1 Samuel 1:11

To know what God wants done (David)
2 Samuel 5:19–23

Thunder and rain (Samuel)
1 Samuel 12:16–17

Forgiveness for adultery and murder (David)
Psalm 51; 2 Samuel 12:16

Wisdom (Solomon)
1 Kings 3:9

A heart wholly devoted to God
Psalm 86:11

Fire from heaven (Elijah)
1 Kings 18:36–38

Success (Jabez)
1 Chronicles 4:10

Protection for their city (Hezekiah)
2 Kings 19:14–19

Strengthened hands (Nehemiah)
Nehemiah 6:9

Revival
Psalm 85:6–7

Protection from Satan (Jesus)
John 17:15

Salvation of the Jews (Paul)
Romans 10:1

To speak God's Word with boldness
(Apostles)
Acts 4:24–30; Ephesians 6:19–20

New believers to receive the Holy Spirit (Peter and John for believers in Samaria)
Acts 8:15

That other believers would do right
2 Corinthians 13:7

That the eyes of one's heart may be opened
Ephesians 1:18

Government leaders
1 Timothy 2:1–2

Good health (John for Gaius)
3 John 1:2

The gospel to be spread
2 Thessalonians 3:1

The Prayer of Jabez

Jabez cried out to the God of Israel, "Oh, that you would bless me and enlarge my territory! Let your hand be with me, and keep me from harm so that I will be free from pain." And God granted his request.

—1 Chronicles 4:10

WHERE DID THEY PRAY?

Outdoors (Abraham's Servant)
Genesis 24:11–12

On the battlefield (Joshua)
Joshua 7:6–9

At the altar (Solomon)
2 Chronicles 6:12–14

In their room (Daniel)
Daniel 6:10

In bed
Psalm 63:6

Inside the belly of a whale (Jonah)
Jonah 2:2–9

On a mountainside (Jesus)
Luke 6:12; 9:28

At the temple (Pharisee and tax collector)
Luke 18:10

From prison (Paul and Silas)
Acts 16:25

On the beach (disciples)
Acts 21:5

WHEN DID THEY PRAY?

At midnight
Psalm 119:62; Acts 16:25

Three times a day (Daniel)
Daniel 6:10

All through the night (Samuel)
1 Samuel 15:11

Every morning
Psalm 5:3

At fixed times daily
Psalm 55:17

Very early in the morning (Jesus)
Mark 1:35

While nearly drowning (Peter)
Matthew 14:30

While being crucified (Thief on the cross)
Luke 23:42

While being martyred (Stephen)
Acts 7:59–60

During a period set apart for prayer
1 Corinthians 7:5

HOW DID THEY PRAY?

Sitting (David)
2 Samuel 7:18

Standing (Solomon)
1 Kings 8:22 (Also Mark 11:25)

Kneeling (Peter)
*Acts 9:40 (Also Daniel 6:10; Ephesians
3:14; 1 Kings 8:54)*

Facing Jerusalem (Daniel)
Daniel 6:10

In whispers
Isaiah 26:16

In silence (Hannah)
1 Samuel 1:13

In a loud voice (Ezra)
Ezra 11:13

Looking up (Jesus)
John 11:41

With hands toward heaven (Solomon)
1 Kings 8:22 (Also Psalm 28:2)

With face to the ground (Jesus)
Matthew 26:39

With bitter weeping (Hezekiah)
Isaiah 38:2–3

With tears and crying (Ezra)
Ezra 10:1 (Also Jesus; Hebrews 5:7)

With joy! (Paul)
Philippians 1:4

As a group (believers)
Acts 1:14

Alone (Jesus)
Matthew 14:23

In unison (believers)
Acts 4:24

Earnestly! (Paul, Silas, and Timothy)
1 Thessalonians 3:10

THE PRAYERS OF JESUS

Jesus took time to pray to God the Father. Jesus "often withdrew to lonely places and prayed" (Luke 5:16) and he would pray for long stretches of time (Luke 6:12).

Jesus . . .

Prayed for his followers.

> *"I pray for them. I am not praying for the world, but for those you have given me, for they are yours."* —John 17:9

Prayed for little children.

> *Then people brought little children to Jesus for him to place his hands on them and pray for them.* —Matthew 19:13

Praised the Father in prayer.

> *At that time Jesus said, "I praise*

you, Father, Lord of heaven and earth … " —Matthew 11:25

Prayed for himself.

After Jesus said this, he looked toward heaven and prayed: "Father, the hour has come. Glorify your Son, that your Son may glorify you." —John 17:1

Prayed for Simon Peter.

"But I have prayed for you, Simon, that your faith may not fail. And when you have turned back, strengthen your brothers." —Luke 22:32

Prayed that his Father's will be done.

"Father, if you are willing, take this cup from me; yet not my will, but yours be done." —Luke 22:42 (Matthew 26:39)

Thanked the Father in prayer.

> *Then Jesus looked up and said, "Father, I thank you that you have heard me."* —John 11:41 (See also Luke 24:30)

Asked the Father to forgive sinners.

> *"Father, forgive them, for they do not know what they are doing."* —Luke 23:34

Prayed with his last words on the cross.

> *Jesus called out with a loud voice, "Father, into your hands I commit my spirit." When he had said this, he breathed his last.* —Luke 23:46

For I know the plans I have for you," declares the Lord, "plans to prosper you and not to harm you, plans to give you hope and a future. Then you will call on me and come and pray to me, and I will listen to you. You will seek me and find me when you seek me with all your heart."

—Jeremiah 29:11–13

You Might Also Like

What the Bible Says about Prayer
ISBN: 9781628622027

What the Bible Says about Forgiveness
ISBN: 9781628622034

What the Bible Says about Money
ISBN: 9781628622041

Following Jesus
ISBN: 9781628622058

Names of God
ISBN: 9781628620863

How to Study the Bible
ISBN: 9781628620856

Book of Psalms
ISBN: 9781628620832

The Love Chapter
ISBN: 9781628620849